Fashions of a Decade
The 1980s

Fashions of a Decade
The 1980s

Vicky Carnegy

CHELSEA HOUSE
PUBLISHERS
An imprint of Infobase Publishing

Chelsea House
An imprint of Infobase Publishing
132 West 31st Street
New York NY 10001

Library of Congress Cataloging-in-Publication Data
Carnegy, Vicky.
    Fashions of a decade. The 1980s/Vicky Carnegy
    p. cm.
    Includes bibliographical references and index
    ISBN-13: 978-0-8160-6724-4
    ISBN-10: 0-8160-6724-4 (alk. paper)
    1. Clothing and dress—History—20th century—Juvenile
    literature. I. Title.
    GT596.C33   2006
    391.00904—dc22   2006049458

Chelsea House books are available at special discounts when
purchased in bulk quantities for businesses, associations,
institutions, or sales promotions. Please call our Special
Sales Department in New York at (212) 967-8800 or
(800) 322-8755.

You can find Chelsea House on the World Wide Web at
http://www.chelseahouse.com

Research for new edition: Kathy Elgin
Editor: Karen Taschek
Text design by Simon Borrough
Cover design by Dorothy M. Preston
Illustrations by Robert Price
Picture Research by Shelley Noronha

This new edition produced for Chelsea House by Bailey
Publishing Associates Ltd.

Printed in China through Morris Press, Ltd.

MPL SB 10 9 8 7 6 5 4 3 2

This book is printed on acid-free paper.

Contents

The 80s

It had to happen. After the swinging sixties and the excesses of 1970s punk rock, there had to be a backlash. It came in the 1980s, with the art of being serious, grown-up, and hardworking carried to the extreme.

But the decade didn't start quite like that. The punk revolution was still in the air, although by 1980, the general trend was to tone down and tame the original punk style. Pop stars like Prince and Boy George, for example, did not look threatening but rather appealing, with their careful makeup and colorful clothes. As the shock effect of outrageous Mohawk hairstyles wore off, even they became simply another form of decoration—just one more fashion. The mood was whimsical and soft, with velvet knickers and short cheerleader skirts. In Britain, romance was in the air with the engagement of Prince Charles and "Lady Di" in February 1981. Their marriage the following July, televised worldwide, fulfilled all expectations. The bride's fairy-tale dress was copied over and over again for less exalted weddings and helped to set the trend for full-blown romantic evening wear. Would the eighties be yet another decade of escapist fantasies?

◀ Prince Charles and his fiancée, "Lady Di," pose for a formal portrait after announcing their engagement. Over the next few years she would be transformed from shy, conventional teenager into international celebrity and fashion icon.

Reagan and Thatcher—The Conservative Years

Conservative Margaret Thatcher, determined to roll back the postwar socialist era, became the British prime minister in May 1979 and remained in power throughout the 1980s. In the United States, her ideological soul mate, Republican Ronald Reagan, won the presidency in November 1980 and again in 1984. Between them, they set the decade's political agenda. Private enterprise was encouraged and rewarded by favorable taxation. State subsidies, whether to help industry or individuals, were cut—deemed self-defeating by encouraging people to remain in poverty rather than lift themselves out of it.

◄ Nancy and Ronald Reagan at their second inauguration ball, January 1985. The first lady was always fashionably turned out in couture outfits, some of which were not entirely suited to a woman of her age.

▼ British prime minister Margaret Thatcher was another example of transformation from dowdy politician to international star. Once she was in power, image consultants gave her wardrobe, hairstyle, makeup— even her voice—a complete makeover. Here she wears her trademark "pussy cat bow" blouse and a suit in the color of the Conservative Party.

▲ The essential accessory for the well-dressed high achiever: an immaculate black Porsche.

► A 1988 advertisement for Hennes, a popular chain store in Europe eager to sell the upwardly mobile image of black suit, white blouse, black briefcase, and red Ferrari.

▼ As the Soviet Union under Gorbachev began to relax, fashion came to the fore. For day wear (*above*), Western-style square shoulders and oversized jackets were in, but a more traditional Russian look (*below*) was preferred for evenings.

Enter the Yuppies

In fact, this mood did not last long, and the decade soon began to show its true colors. Just as the miniskirted teenage girl became the symbol of the sixties, so the well-tailored young executive, quickly dubbed a "yuppie," summed up the eighties' spirit of hard work and individual responsibility.

This was not just a whim of fashion but a widespread social trend. The election of Ronald Reagan as president in 1980 ushered in a new decade in which it became fashionable to make money and dress well. The Reagans put in motion a fast social whirl, centered around the White House, with smart fund-raising luncheons and evening charity affairs. Just as Ronald Reagan's successful election bid against Jimmy Carter had set a new political tone, so Nancy Reagan's designer wardrobe was a total contrast to the informal style of former first lady Rosalynn Carter. It was now "in" to celebrate success in business or politics conspicuously, with fashionable clothes and accessories. And it was not just in the West that these values were encouraged. The USSR, with Mikhail Gorbachev at the helm, saw the beginnings of some forms of private enterprise, with profit considered a healthy incentive.

The election of sixty-nine-year-old Ronald Reagan was also very much in tune with the demographic changes taking place in North America and Western Europe. Teenagers, if not exactly a dying breed, were dwindling in number as the effects of birth control and marriage at a later age took effect. Youth culture no longer dominated the scene. These changes began to affect fashions as designers—and, more importantly, their financial backers—realized money was no longer to be made by aiming at the teenage market. The people they needed to attract were the older professionals, who were not only increasing in number but also had the extra income to spend on expensive clothing. Fashion had to become serious and recognize that this new breed of consumer did not want gimmicks but clothes that could see them through one business meeting after another.

Designer Shopping

Calvin Klein, Giorgio Armani, and Ralph Lauren targeted their clothes and accessories at this new emerging group and became three of the most

successful fashion emperors of the decade. They spearheaded a "total look" style of shopping, providing their busy customers with everything they needed, from underwear to overcoats, under one designer label. By the end of the decade, designer-manufacturer Donna Karan was being called "the queen of 7th Avenue" for her toned-down, working women's high-style, yet comfortable clothing and accessories.

Many large department stores were rearranged to cater to this new way of merchandising. Inside the stores, you no longer looked for the skirt or dress section but went straight to the designer boutique of your choice to add another item to your well-coordinated wardrobe. This at least was the ideal, but many a shopper must have cursed as she made her way from designer boutique to designer boutique in search of a simple item of clothing. Designer accessories, like Gucci handbags and Rolex watches, became another important status symbol for the "designer shopper."

▲Benetton advertising was often controversial, promoting fashion through images more usually associated with hard news reporting, but their less provocative ads promoted a unisex, multiracial image in tune with their colorful, jaunty clothing.

Chain stores for the younger buyer also adopted this approach. The Italian group Benetton, for example, which had franchises in fifty-seven countries, was enormously successful with its instantly recognizable coordinated separates. Even sport and leisure wear came under the influence of designer labels and coordinating shapes and colors. It was not enough to stay in shape—you needed to look good while doing so. On the ski slopes, the styles and colors of ski pants changed each season and ski boots themselves became more complex and high tech every year. Leotards for workout sessions became high fashion, and trainers had to sport a big-name label like Nike or Reebok to be in fashion. Even the Olympics were almost as much about style as sport, with the top athletes competing in figure-hugging outfits, not to mention all the razzmatazz of the opening ceremonies.

The 1980s also saw the wearing of sneakers move from the playing field, running track, and health club onto the feet of thousands of working women. Most notably, the widely publicized 1980 New York City transit strike resulted in the popular acceptance of running shoes for the long walk to work. The style quickly gained acceptance, and it became commonplace to see otherwise impeccably groomed working women wearing running shoes for getting to and from their jobs. It was a rare eighties woman—or man—who did not own at least one pair of these comfortable shoes.

▲Even when the transit strike was over, many commuters realized that continuing to walk, run, or cycle to work could be a useful part of their fitness routine, saving time in the gym. As a result, sneakers became more fashionable in design.

Gorbachev

Mikhail Sergeyevitch Gorbachev became the leader of the Soviet Union on March 11, 1985, at age fifty-four. Gorbachev's relative youth promised change after years of stagnation under Leonid Brezhnev and his short-lived successors, Yuri Andropov and Konstantin Chernenko. The pace and extent of reform caught the imagination of the world. *Glasnost* (openness) and *perestroika* (restructuring) became part of the international vocabulary as Gorbachev began to loosen the state's iron grip on the economy, allowed the Soviet media hitherto unthinkable freedom, and introduced a measure of democracy. Traditional Marxist-Leninist ideology and history were revised in a way unprecedented since the 1917 revolution. Unfreezing the Cold War in dramatic style, Gorbachev signed a nuclear arms reduction agreement with the United States. But at home, a reluctant and powerful bureaucracy and continual shortages of basic goods remained threats to his success.

▲East meets West in contrasting styles of summit diplomacy dressing. Raisa Gorbachev had an understated elegance sharply at odds with Nancy Reagan's hard-edged designer style.

◄ His-and-hers Rolex watches: the defining symbol of the yuppie couple.

►A smart patent-and-gilt handbag from the early eighties.

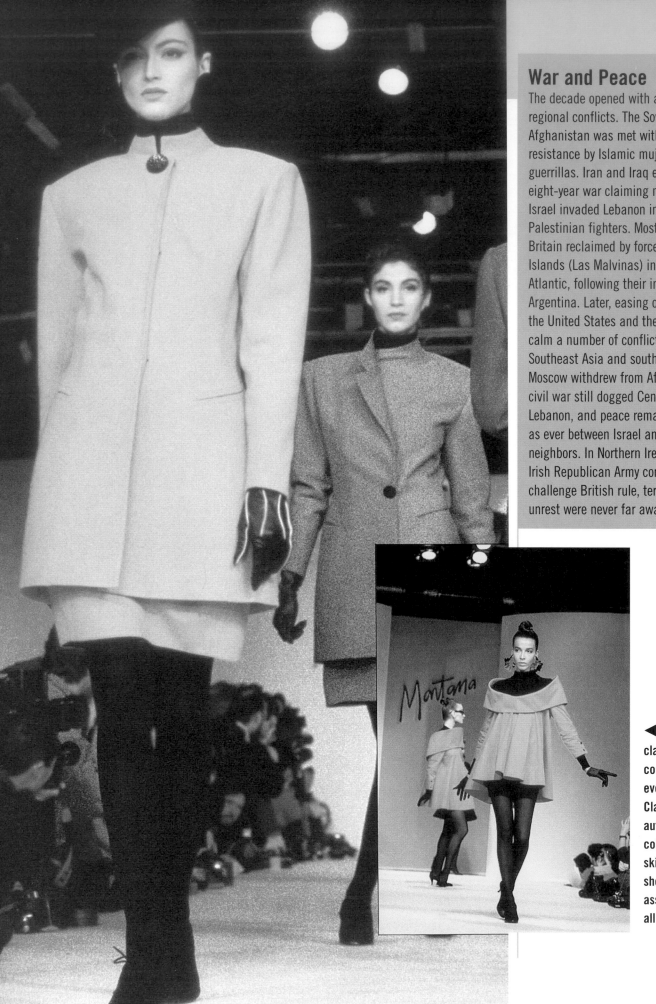

War and Peace

The decade opened with a rash of bitter regional conflicts. The Soviet occupation of Afghanistan was met with determined resistance by Islamic mujahideen guerrillas. Iran and Iraq embarked on an eight-year war claiming millions of lives. Israel invaded Lebanon in 1982 to root out Palestinian fighters. Most bizarre of all, Britain reclaimed by force the tiny Falkland Islands (Las Malvinas) in the South Atlantic, following their invasion by Argentina. Later, easing of tension between the United States and the USSR helped calm a number of conflicts, notably in Southeast Asia and southern Africa. Moscow withdrew from Afghanistan. But civil war still dogged Central America and Lebanon, and peace remained as elusive as ever between Israel and its Arab neighbors. In Northern Ireland, where the Irish Republican Army continued to challenge British rule, terrorism and civil unrest were never far away.

◄ Day and Night: classic eighties couture for day and evening wear from Claude Montana's autumn 1987 collection. Short skirts, wide shoulders, and assertive lines link all these designs.

Politics and Sport

Politics dogged the steps of the Olympic movement when the 1980 and 1984 games were marred by superpower squabbling. President Jimmy Carter tried to organize a full-scale boycott of the 1980 Moscow Olympics in protest of the Soviet invasion of Afghanistan earlier that year, but in the end, the only significant athletic powers not to turn up were the United States, West Germany, and Kenya. Four years later, in a tit-for-tat response, the Soviet Union led a boycott of the Los Angeles games by most of the Eastern Bloc. Superpower friendship ensured a full turnout for the 1988 games in Seoul, South Korea, however, and the games were a great success, despite scandals over the use of drugs by leading athletes.

◀ The opening ceremony of the Olympic Games in Seoul, South Korea, in 1988 gave the world a glimpse into an unfamiliar culture.

▲ Dressed for success: Michael Jackson on his way to receive a Grammy Award in 1984.

New Men?

The male image went through some interesting changes in the eighties. The beginning of the decade saw a fantastic peacock look in some quarters, drawing very much on the early-nineteenth-century dandy in its use of silks and velvets. An absurdly overblown version was taken up by pop stars like Boy George, Prince, and Michael Jackson, with lavish use of makeup and wild hairstyles. While women in the 1970s had been fighting to promote a stronger, more powerful image within a male-dominated world, in the early eighties, some men seemed to be struggling to create a sympathetic, caring, and even beautiful new image for themselves. The rise in popularity of the yuppie look pointed male fashion in a new direction, with more conservatively styled suits and ties becoming high fashion even for youngsters.

On the surface, this looked like a return to the familiar twentieth-century male tradition—but a new spirit was afoot. Care was the key word. Men were increasingly concerned about their appearance and about looking good. Success was not just reflected in salary but in a whole lifestyle, encompassing car, house, clothing, and body. Even if you were glued to the computer screen twelve hours at a time, a healthy tan and sleek, conservative appearance were the order of the day. Great interest was taken in the smaller details of clothing, and conversations about the finer points of pleats and cuffs were not uncommon.

Even underwear became controversial, with debates over the merits and demerits of boxer shorts, bikini briefs, and jockey shorts. Male beauty products finally started to take off as the rugged male image of the seventies gave way to something altogether smoother and more refined. More aftershave, more hair products, and even makeup were sold. If you couldn't keep up a tan naturally, you could at least fake it and not be ashamed of doing so.

◀ Rapper Marky Mark of the Funky Bunch was one of the first celebrities to model Calvin Klein underwear for men. These images were seen everywhere, from the subway to mile-high billboards in the street.

▶Yves Saint Laurent's best-selling cologne evoked an image of male beauty from the classical world—*kouros* is Greek for "adolescent youth." Like him, eighties man was perfectly proportioned, clean-shaven, toned, and tan.

▼This early Apple computer may have lacked the design chic of later models, but it was a miracle of speed in the early eighties.

New Technological Age

The post-industrial age of computer-based technology became a reality in the 1980s. Perhaps the most dramatic change came in the office, with the desktop personal computer, first pioneered by the American company Apple. It was made possible by condensing large amounts of computing capacity into tiny silicon microchips. Chips were also used to control industrial robots, which were increasingly replacing human labor in areas like car manufacturing. Chips, satellites, and other technologies like digital encoding and fiber optics transformed telecommunications, with computer, telephone, and television networks spreading all over the world. For the home consumer, new technology meant home computers, video-cassette recorders, compact discs, and the promise of big-screen high definition television.

THE SPIRIT OF CONQUEST

KOUROS
EAU DE TOILETTE

Saint Laurent

New Women

Just as men were using old female tricks to perk up their appearance, so women were at the old game of stealing from the male wardrobe and adapting men's clothing to their needs. This was by no means surprising, as more and more women became accepted in high-status jobs. Although the average female earned less than her male counterpart, the female executive was very much a part of the eighties. Her office outfit borrowed from traditional menswear, with various styles of skirt and jacket becoming standard. Shoulder pads added width to the female form and lent an air of authority. Perhaps even more than men, women in successful careers had to look good as well as be good at their jobs and exude an aura of success. In the United States, 1984 vice-presidential candidate Geraldine Ferraro's style of "power dressing" was a key factor in her political success, while British prime minister Margaret Thatcher paid a considerable amount of attention to her appearance, using her manner and dress as one of her tools to win confidence—and elections. In a 1985 interview, Thatcher admitted to being a keen reader of *Vogue* magazine. In contrast, the British opposition parties never found anyone, male or female, with a comparable style to challenge her.

Islam

The power of the Muslim religion burst on the Western world in January 1979 with the overthrow of the Shah of Iran, a long-standing ally of the United States. He was swept away on a tide of Islamic fundamentalism headed by Ayatollah Ruholla Khomeini, who, until his death in 1989, symbolized a worldwide resurgence of Islamic consciousness. The intensity of feeling against the West was marked by the holding of US embassy hostages in Tehran for more than a year and, in Lebanon, multiple kidnappings of foreigners and attacks against diplomats and soldiers. In Iran, Western dress for women was frowned on and traditional Islamic costume encouraged as a counter to the influence of the "Great Satan"— the United States.

▲ Iranian women wearing the traditional, all-enveloping chador consider a wall poster of the Ayatollah Khomeini.

◀ Young professional women demanded smart, sophisticated clothing that reminded everyone they were a force to be reckoned with.

▲ A 1984 edition of *The Face*, best-selling music-and-lifestyle magazine on both sides of the Atlantic.

◀ Bodybuilding—for both sexes—was an eighties craze. Bodybuilders shared with power dressers the desire to be noticed and to appear commanding, and confident in all situations.

Politics and the Environment

In April 1986, a terrifying explosion at the Chernobyl nuclear reactor near Kiev in Ukraine focused the growing concern about man-made threats to the world environment. The Green Party in West Germany and groups like Greenpeace and Friends of the Earth had led the way, but now environmental issues were taken up by political parties of all colors. Campaigns highlighted the possible threat of global warming—the greenhouse effect—supposedly caused by burning fossil fuels, the destruction of rain forests, depletion of the protective ozone layer by chemical emissions, and wide-scale industrial pollution. The dilemma, especially for the developing world, was how to balance environmental protection with economic growth.

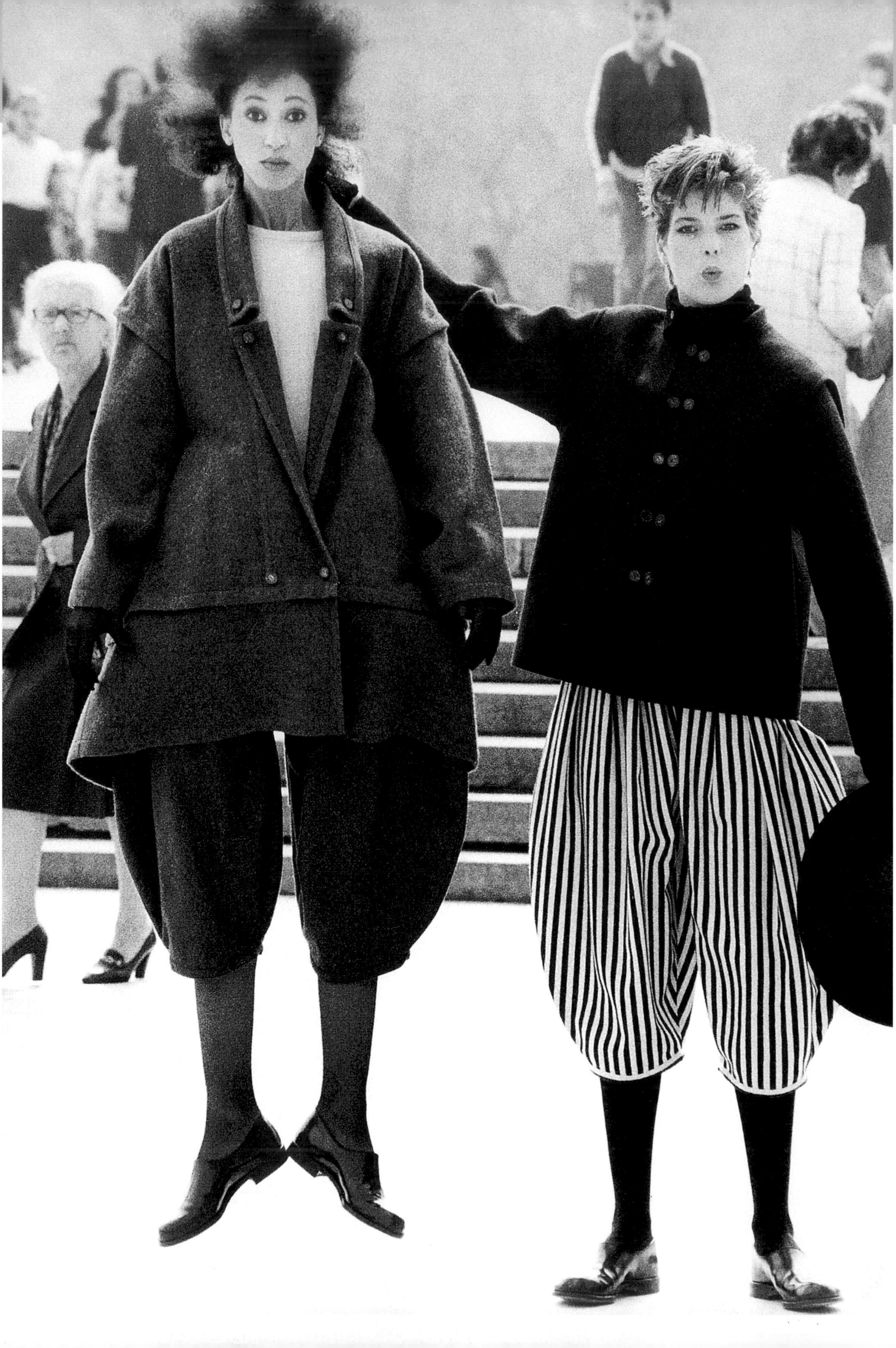

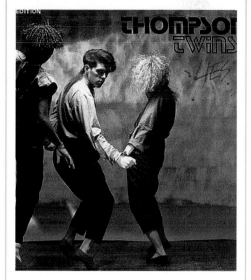

▲Breakout: the Thompson Twins made it big in 1983, taking on board the new dress style from Japan.

◀ The playful nature of Rei Kawakubo's designs for 1980 concealed the careful cutting and tailoring needed to achieve their asymmetrical effect.

▶A typically elegant Armani ensemble from 1985, with houndstooth-check pants and discreetly beaded top.

East Meets West

The most original ideas of the eighties came from Japanese designers, who showed another way of mixing up the sexes and challenged all the accepted ideas of femininity. The "new" dressing pioneered by Rei Kawakubo of Comme des Garçons and Yohji Yamamoto totally disguised the shape of the body beneath layers of clothing that were often geometric and asymmetric in shape. These clothes rejected traditional Western notions of women's clothes—they were neither obviously feminine nor conventionally decorative. Their unglamorous, functional nature appeared radical to Western eyes, although many of the designs were firmly rooted in Japanese tradition and could almost be seen as a homage to the country's past and a challenge to the increased Western influence there. Men and women were dressed in carefully constructed shapes, echoing kimonos or the simpler shapes of karate jackets.

In the West, the new designs struck an immediate chord with the young, who were drawn to these stark, severe designs. Black, the color most favored by the Japanese designers, became a widespread uniform for youth. There was an undercurrent of violence in some of the designs, with torn and slashed cloth wrapped around the body—although in a very stylized way, in contrast to the anarchic style of punk. Some saw in this a sidelong comment on a decade when disasters, both natural and man-made, might be portents of the end of the world.

Into the Nineties

The last years of the eighties saw a relaxation in all areas of fashion. The real peaks of "yuppiness" had passed, and a sense of nostalgia for the recent past was setting in. In music, the "House" scene emerged in Chicago—dance music that harked back to seventies disco for inspiration and was in sharp contrast to the politically conscious and rhythmically complex rap and hip-hop movements. House soon went worldwide, changing along the way. In Britain, it evolved into the much touted "Acid House" craze—famous for yellow smiley-face badges and notoriously linked with the new synthetic drug Ecstasy. It looked as if a purely fun-loving mood was going to take over.

As so often happens in fashion, the mood of the streets was taken up and transformed by the big-name designers. The collections of autumn 1988 and spring 1989 were full of fringes, beads, and flowers, and the party mood of the revelers was captured in expensive high fashion. Even Rei Kawakubo abandoned black, introducing pink rosebuds on shirts for men and pale blue trousers. Exclusive shops sold expensive jeans with their knees carefully ripped. Perhaps unsure how to attack the coming decade, some designers were looking back for inspiration and in doing so creating a new fashion mood in which to enter the nineties.

▲Power dressing in action: Geraldine Ferraro on the campaign trail.

▶Annie Lennox, formerly of the Eurythmics, was just one of the women in the music world who challenged conventional ideas of feminine dressing.

Debt and Famine

In the 1970s, the West's commercial banks loaned huge amounts of money to developing countries. A decade later, unexpectedly high interest rates and economic recession made repayment difficult or impossible for a number of nations. Debt crisis in South America and sub-Saharan Africa threatened the stability of the world's banking and financial systems, and the livelihoods of millions in debtor countries were stretched to the breaking point by the burden of debt. The biggest sums were owed by Brazil and Mexico, but Africa, owing a total of $200 billion, saw the most desperate results as near-bankrupt nations were simultaneously hit by drought, causing widespread famine and poverty. Western creditors debated solutions, but throughout the 1980s, the net flow of funds continued from poor to rich nations.

Live Aid

July 7, 1985: probably the most star-studded assembly of rock musicians ever played in satellite-linked concerts broadcast on television around the world to aid the millions suffering from famine in Ethiopia and other sub-Saharan African nations. The man behind it was the unkempt but passionately articulate Irish rock star Bob Geldof. His efforts sparked a tide of similar events throughout the rest of the decade.

◀ After the success of Live Aid, fashion jumped on the bandwagon in 1986. Here Grace Jones, Marie Helvin, and Jerry Hall get ready for Fashion Aid.

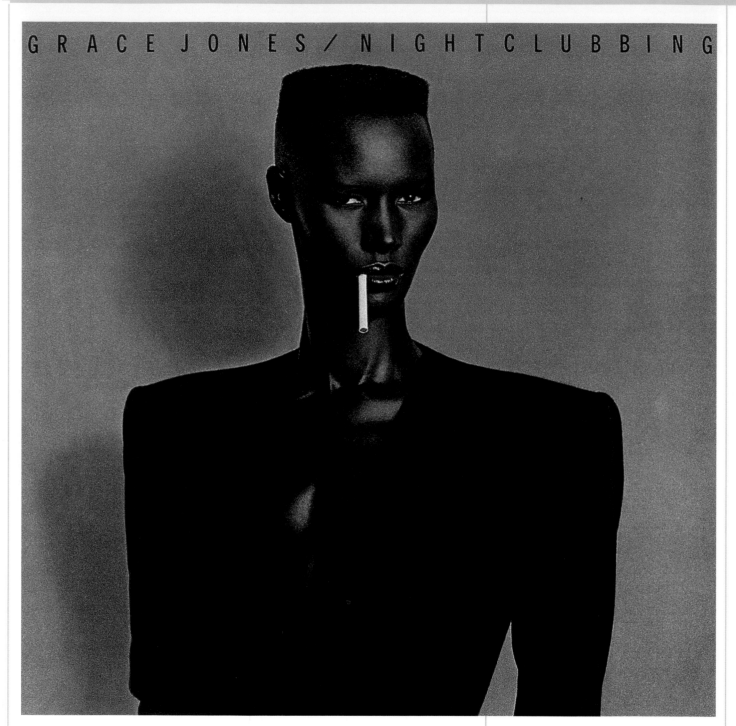

GRACE JONES / NIGHTCLUBBING

▲ Grace Jones played with male-female stereotyping, her androgynous image perfectly in tune with the rather masculine dress style of the eighties. Like David Bowie, she adopted various stage personas, each with outlandish costumes.

▶ Men were becoming more aware of what women had always known—that careful choice of accessories could improve any outfit. Sales of ties, belts, cufflinks and even handbags increased hugely as men became more image conscious.

China

While Mikhail Gorbachev was grabbing the headlines for his political reforms in the Soviet Union, China, the twentieth century's other great Communist power, was undergoing equally dramatic economic reform under Deng Xiaoping. Private enterprise and foreign investment were encouraged, leading to a more dynamic economy, although problems arose with inflation. These changes led to growing pressure, especially among students, for greater political freedom. Ironically, a visit by Mr. Gorbachev in 1989 was the focus for huge popular demonstrations, with thousands thronging Tiananmen Square in Beijing. On June 4, in a bloody reaction that shocked a world watching on TV, the Red Army brutally crushed the protests. Moderates in government were purged as Deng ruthlessly reasserted the supremacy of the party.

AIDS

A new fatal illness, transmitted through blood and body fluids, AIDS was detected early in the decade in big American cities but appeared to have come from Africa, where its effects were worst. Characterized by an inability to resist even minor infections—the acronym stands for acquired immune deficiency syndrome—it was at first mistakenly labeled an exclusively homosexual problem. Scientists began researching AIDS, but the public was initially given little accurate information to help prevent its spread or to allay spiraling rumors and scare stories. By 1985, the World Health Organization reported that AIDS had reached epidemic proportions. Several noted fashion designers died from the disease —including Perry Ellis, Willy Smith, and expatriate American Patrick Kelly. The actor Rock Hudson and the entertainer Liberace were among those in the public eye to be struck down. By the end of the decade, the exact cause and progression of the disease were still unknown and no cure had been found.

◀ Pro-democracy demonstrators occupy Tiananmen Square, Beijing, in May 1989.

◀ AIDS awareness posters produced in the mid-eighties.

▶ A sixties-style printed jacket and miniskirt teamed with Edwardian lacy top, gloves, and tights - this may be one of Madonna's more restrained outfits, but the highly original mixture of styles prefigures the layered Bohemian look of the nineties.

◄ Unusual combinations of leather and wool, color, and cut identify this 1988 mini by Christian Lacroix.

◀ ▶Sexy and feminine at the same time, mini-crinolines in various styles, colors, and textures were the highlight of Vivienne Westwood's 1985 collection.

Romantics, Pirates, and Princes

A New Romance

Forget black plastic sacks, safety pin earrings, and rags and tatters, even of the Zandra Rhodes variety. In 1980, most young people had had enough of the revolution and wanted to sink into nostalgia and the cozy comfort of ribbons and bows. The American hostages were still in Iran, the Soviet Union had just invaded Afghanistan, and European unemployment was rising at an alarming rate. Fashion pushed all this to one side and looked back to a different age of silks and velvets, swashbuckling pirates, and handsome highwaymen.

Vivienne Westwood, first lady of punk, changed the name of her King's Road shop in London from Seditionaries to World's End and settled down to producing her New Romantic and Pirate looks, which were greeted with enthusiasm. With leggings and long, soft boots falling around the ankles, they recalled Errol Flynn movies of the 1930s and 1940s and seemed totally removed from the harsher realities of life.

▶Prince in a still from the 1984 movie *Purple Rain*. He made sure that the swashbuckling look stayed in fashion right through the decade.

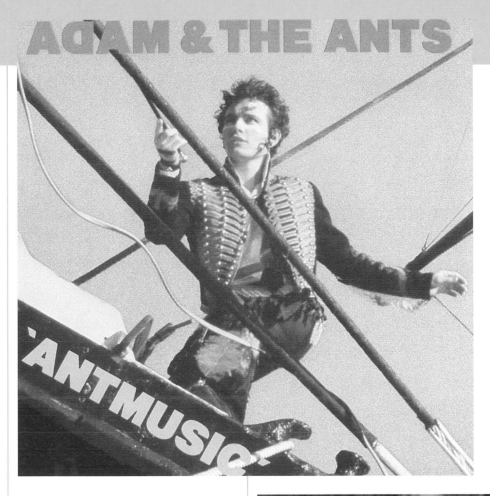

The pop world caught on to the idea quickly. Prince, in his velvets and laces, actually looked the part his name conjured up. Kid Creole and the Coconuts dressed up as "Tropical Gangsters." Michael Jackson simply went on being himself. Adam and the Ants reflected the mood perfectly with the video of their 1981 hit single "Stand and Deliver." Dressed up as a dashing eighteenth-century highwayman, Adam Ant crashed into a hall of revelers in full romantic dress. Boy George, with his overdone makeup and outrageous costumes, added fantasy and fun to the scene rather than provoking any challenge to conventional society.

▲King of the Wild Frontier: Adam Ant poses for the cover of his 1980 hit single "Ant Music."

►Another Westwood creation, heralding the New Romantics look.

A True Romance

Somewhere a fairy tale had to justify all this. The British royal family provided it with the marriage of Prince Charles, the heir to the throne, to the young and charming Lady Diana Spencer. He could not compete with the rock stars, but "Lady Di" soon became the darling of the world's media. The pageantry of the royal wedding in July 1981 seemed scarcely a part of the twentieth century.

The bride, in a full-skirted dress designed by the then relatively unknown Emanuels, fulfilled all romantic expectations. Within hours of its first showing on television, the dress had been copied and placed in the windows of major department stores, ready for other romantic brides to order.

▲ However hard-edged the eighties were going to be, every little girl's fairy tale came true in 1981 with the royal wedding.

▲ Boy George was a performer who played with people's expectations of sexual and social behavior. Curiously, despite his experiments with makeup, ribbons, and braided hair, few people found him objectionable.

▶ Sloane Rangers got their name from Sloane Square, at the end of King's Road in London's fashionable Chelsea district.

▼ The Burberry trench coat had been enjoying classic status as country wear since the middle of the nineteenth century.

Class Comes Out

The royal romance and the generally softer mood of fashion brought into prominence the style of an unlikely set of people. Known as "preppies" in the United States and "Sloane Rangers" in Britain, their image was of established and successful families. The clothes they wore were usually timeless classics like kilts and cashmere twin sets, tweed jackets and trousers usually associated with country pursuits.

Robust country wear, like that provided by L. L. Bean, was what you wore for leisure. Even if you had to stay in the city for the weekend, you could still dress as if you were about to go off riding, fishing, or hunting. Tradition was fashionable, with much use of tweed, plaids, and intricate hand knits. Soft mixtures of greens and purples echoed country landscapes and brought a breath of fresh air into the town. The look was too static and staid to remain high fashion for long, however, and a sharper, more aggressive silhouette soon emerged.

Power Dressing: The City Slicker and the New Woman

Enter the Yuppies

An important new market for designer clothes was tapped in the 1980s: men and women in their twenties and early thirties in high-paying jobs. Hard work was fashionable and a large salary something to be shown off in expensive cars and designer clothes. European companies were increasingly abandoning their more traditional approach to recruitment and adopting the American practice of rewarding young talent fast with good jobs and good salaries. The term *yuppie*—standing for "young urban professional"—was coined to describe the phenomenon. While few would admit to being one, the "yuppie" market became an important target for advertisers selling everything from cars to instant coffee by portraying a wealthy, successful, hardworking but young lifestyle.

The Aggressive Silhouette

The look produced by designers in the early 1980s for this market was essentially based on the male silhouette. Wide shoulders were key, emphasized with pads. For daytime, the suit was essential for both the working man and woman. His was, typically, double breasted and with front-pleated trousers, creating a broad, powerful image. For her, the jacket was worn over a safe, on– or below-the-knee-length narrow skirt. The classic Armani jacket, hanging loosely from wide shoulders, disguised the waist and narrowed the hips, leaving hair, makeup, and legs to proclaim femininity.

In contrast to the aggressive exterior, many women began to wear frilly feminine lingerie, and companies like Victoria's Secret capitalized on the market for these garments.

▲The real-life look of classic Armani, generously cut and draped.

► The preferred working uniform of the eighties male. Double-breasted, square-cut tailoring suggested substance, strength—and, of course, money.

Television helped spread the power dressing message. Stars like *(right)* Joan Collins in *Dynasty*, Linda Gray in *Dallas (below)* and *(above)* Corbin Bernsen in *LA Law* played characters who, although often unscrupulous in their behavior, took glamour and high achieving to the ultimate degree.

Glamour was kept for evenings. The increasing popularity of formal events like charity balls was an opportunity for female display, while men had a ready uniform in the dinner jacket or tuxedo.

Beneath the clothes, the body, too, was being molded into a powerful form. Exercise in the 1970s had concentrated on slimming down the figure, but in the early 1980s bodybuilding and exercise machines became the fashionable way to stay in shape. The goal, for women as well as for men, was a strong, powerful figure. The most extreme professional female bodybuilders upset all conventional ideas of the female form, echoing the rejection of the traditional feminine role by the successful businesswoman. In 1983, Calvin Klein summed up this mood, perhaps light-heartedly, with his jockey shorts for women. They proved to be a best seller.

Designer Lifestyle

Calvin Klein and Ralph Lauren in New York, and Giorgio Armani in Milan, worked this "yuppie" market to the hilt. They realized the importance of creating and controlling the right image for their clothes through their own advertising, rather than leaving it to fashion editors to bring the clothes to the buyers' notice. They could provide a total look, not to be mixed with anyone else's designs. They also lived the lifestyle they designed for, being as much astute and successful businessmen as creative designers. The importance of hitting the right image was shown by the success of German designer Hugo Boss, whose sales soared by 21 percent when his suits were worn by television actors starring in *Miami Vice* and *LA Law*. Suddenly Boss was selling not just a beautifully tailored suit but an exciting and successful image.

Boom or Bust?

For a short while after the 1987 stock market crash, it seemed as if the yuppie look and lifestyle were going into retreat. But this never quite happened. The fashionably aggressive look certainly softened, with shoulder pads for women becoming less important and men's suits slimmer in line. But the overall look remained important throughout the eighties, with the business suit for men and women an important fashion item. The designer empires built on this market continued to flourish and looked set to expand in the 1990s.

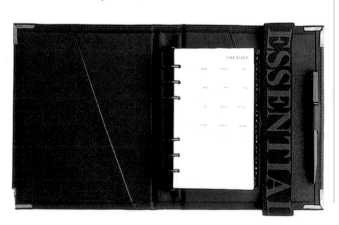

▶ **Work never stops, and time is money. A personal organizer** *(left)* **and mobile phone** *(right)* **became the symbols of the urban professional's way of life, although the phone would soon be a fraction of its 1980s size.**

◀ Princess Diana began the eighties as a fairy-tale bride (see page 30), but ended them dressed as a chic go-getter.

▶ Victoria's Secret soon cornered the market in comfortable but sexy lingerie for the up-and-coming executive.

Cut, Shape, and Drape

▲ Japanese designer Yohji Yamamoto with the models who showed his spring 1986 collection.

Invasion from the East

In 1981, the Japanese really came to town. Rei Kawakubo of Comme des Garçons presented her collection in Paris. Not yet part of the accepted fashion scene, she showed her clothes on hangers at the Hotel Intercontinental in Paris, and the fashion editors flocked to see them. Soon, Yohji Yamamoto was opening a boutique in Les Halles, Paris. Already well established in Japan, these designers now set out to conquer the West with their own unusual style.

Not everyone was enthusiastic. The prestigious *Women's Wear Daily* labeled their image "the Hiroshima bag lady look." Others, though, were completely won over by a style that ran against all the current high-fashion rules. Their clothes seemed to start from a totally different basis from those of traditional Western designers. Instead of using the body as the basic form, these garments could completely disguise the person beneath and were sometimes more like sculpture in their exaggerated shapes and textures. They also acted as

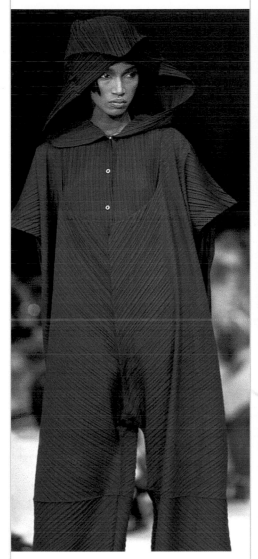

▲This beautifully styled and textured Issey Miyake design for 1989 successfully confuses our normal ideas about shape and proportion.

▲ Romeo Gigli provides another interpretation of cut and shape that is, in its own way, as unexpected as the designs from Japan.

a reminder that fashion developed very differently in other parts of the world.

Kawakubo's work in particular, although stylized as part of the "new" dressing and claiming to be influenced by nothing from the past, did echo traditional Japanese motifs.

A Look to Live In ...

Both Kawakubo and Yamamoto claimed to be making functional clothing for working people rather than for the super-rich and leisured. Certainly, their unusual shapes and heavy use of black were popular with the young. "There is nothing so boring as a neat and tidy look" was printed on the labels of Yamamoto's inexpensive collection, an idea almost bound to appeal. In fact, their garments required a good deal of dedication to wear and could be tricky to get in and out of. The look was meant to be total and never to be mixed up with other designers' work. These clothes were sold only in carefully controlled retail shops that could guarantee to carry a full range of the designs, and both designers were known for the attention they paid to the architectural detail of their own boutiques. In total contrast to the often multi-layered and heavily textured garments, the shops were sparse and minimalist.

▲ Another lesson from the Japanese taught us that "less is more." Stores like this Comme des Garçons retail outlet were minimal in the extreme and at first intimidated prospective shoppers.

▼Asymmetric, tangled, draped and distressed—the Comme des Garçons look was unmistakable.

Reply from the West

It took three years for any Western designer to come up with such a new and challenging look. Then in 1984, Romeo Gigli in Milan suddenly produced his softly draped "Italian Madonnas," which, again, were a total contrast to all the current looks. In London, young fashion student John Galliano became instantly famous for his "Les Incroyables" collection.

Gigli and Galliano used ideas from the past to create a new and challenging image, this time one more easily understood by Western eyes. The high-waisted silhouette did not disguise the body underneath but instead revealed its natural contours. Set against the very powerful, formal image of the city slicker, this was as much of a shock as the asymmetrical layers of Yamamoto.

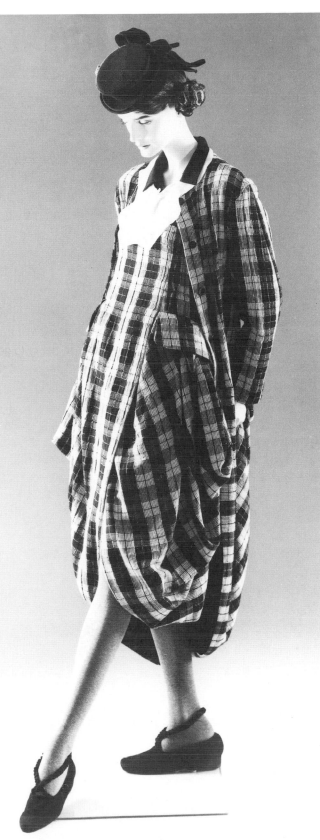

▲ ►The arch-romantic John Galliano in two moods: *(right)* a seriously wearable day dress and *(above)* a dazzling confection of silk ruffles for evening wear.

Bizarre and Absurd

The Wild Side

Why do we do it? Fashion is crazy. Few of the clothes we pull on every day are made just to keep us warm or cool or dry—or even comfortable. Even fewer of the clothes in the glossy magazines have anything to do with these qualities. We squeeze ourselves into shapes, change from short skirts to long or from tight jeans to baggy pants and then, in a matter of months, are ready to move on yet again to something new.

The clothes shown on the catwalks by major designers both reflect this urge for change and help to fuel it. Some of the wildest ideas may never be worn in the street, but they stimulate thought and act as a challenge. In the 1980s, Jean Paul Gaultier showed a range of men's skirts. If women can wear pants, what is so odd about men in skirts? Christian Lacroix deliberately set out to amuse and intrigue with his fantasy shapes and rich decoration. Vivienne Westwood attacked the wide-shouldered, slim-hipped silhouette of the 1980s female executive with her "mini-crinolines," which influenced countless party dresses even if her original design remained too bold and strong for the mass market.

Escape!

Was reality just too hard to take? Throughout the eighties, flights to fantasy-land were always available. Space and adventure films were wildly popular and provided an easy way of forgetting about life's problems. In the pop world, two megastars, Michael Jackson and Madonna, fueled their success by making their public images more weird and wonderful each month. Madonna's look-alike fan club had a hard task keeping up with each change.

The more adventurous, however, were not satisfied by mere copying. There was a thriving nightclub scene for those who wanted to create their own fantasy. To get into the best clubs, it was not enough to have money; you had to have "style"—and the right style for each changing week. Clubs were notorious for a while, then abandoned by anyone at all in the know.

The nightclub scene was brought onto the runways by designers like Patricia Field, John Galliano, and the Body Map team. Sometimes adored by the fashion press, at other

▲They only come out at night: bright young things clubbing at New York's Palladium.

▲ Jean Paul Gaultier's skirts for men—one revolutionary idea that didn't catch on.

▶The original material girl. The many incarnations of Madonna's stage persona took some of the street fashions of the early eighties to the limit.

Karl Lagerfeld is fond of introducing everyday shapes and objects into his designs, often creating a surreal effect in the style of Schiaparelli, back in the thirties. Another design from 1983 featured a shower that sent glittering "spray" down the model's back.

times detested for their weird, amateurish approach, they could at least be relied on to be different. The shows were often more like theater, presented with long and sometimes incomprehensible titles and including friends and followers as well as professional models.

Secret Outlets

The more timid had an easier way to add just a hint of the fantastic to their lives from the explosion of small accessories covered with exotic and ridiculous motifs. Socks and underpants were the two main targets to be covered by all sorts of patterns from black-and-white keyboards to Mickey Mouse. The success of the 1989 film *Batman* led to a period of total Batmania, with bats appearing on everything from boxer shorts to toddlers' sweatshirts.

◄ Amid all the severity of eighties power dressing, the ever-inventive Vivienne Westwood could always be counted on to come up with something outrageous.

Hip-hop, House, and After

▼Afrikaa Bambaata and Soulsonic Force—African American break-dancing superheroes.

Get Up Offa That Thing

By 1981, the trend was clear—the eighties were set to be the decade of dance music. The discos of the seventies re-emerged as the places where street sounds and street fashions were made. New York clubs led the way, with DJs like Larry Levan of the Paradise Garage and "Jellybean" Benitez of the Funhouse mixing the sounds and getting involved in the production side as well—Madonna was one of Benitez's early discoveries. But most of the new dance floor stars were African American artists: Afrikaa Bambaata, Grandmaster Flash and the Furious Five, Planet Patrol, Run DMC.

Meanwhile, soul music's established dance floor fillers—James Brown, Hamilton Bohannon—gained a new lease on life, while jazz superstar Herbie Hancock re-emerged as king of the dance floor with the smash hit "Rockit."

Serious dancing meant a serious dance style—clothes that were eye catching but also comfortable to move in. In 1982 and 1983 the look might be short, black, studded-leather jackets or denims mixed with "spray-on" pants for the girls, baggy drawstring pants or cutoff shorts on hot nights for the boys. Athletes' sweatbands at the wrists marked the really devoted dancers; sneakers or similar footwear were a must.

Body Popping

By 1984, the dance floor had been taken over by the electrobeat sound—records built around the drum machine and synthesizer, the words usually rapped instead of sung. Break dancing had emerged as an international craze—falling on your back ("body slam"), spinning on your back ("helicopter"), even spinning on one hand ("one-hand glide"). Break dancers formed teams or "crews," held street shows, and competed in championships, national and international. But you had to be young and very fit.

The look was minimalist. Sportswear became a necessity: nothing else could stand up to the wear and tear of bodypopping. Labels became crucial—

▲Two-way traffic—King Sunny Ade and his African Beats mix Western and West African styles on a 1983 record jacket.

▲For break dancing, loose sportswear was the only option, and if you wanted to spin on your head, a hooded sweatshirt was a must.

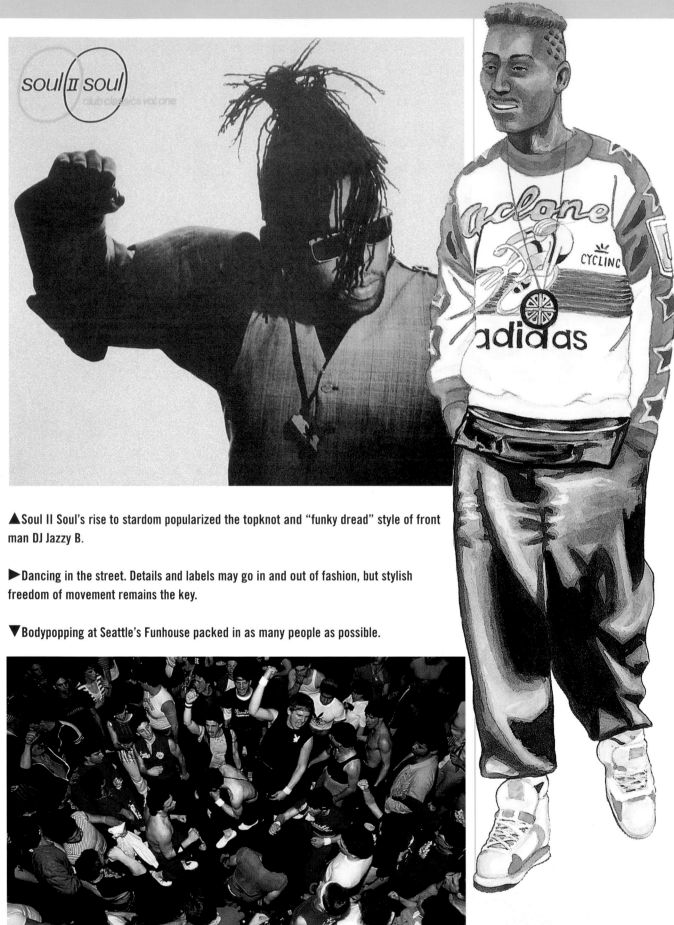

▲Soul II Soul's rise to stardom popularized the topknot and "funky dread" style of front man DJ Jazzy B.

►Dancing in the street. Details and labels may go in and out of fashion, but stylish freedom of movement remains the key.

▼Bodypopping at Seattle's Funhouse packed in as many people as possible.

▼Public Enemy came to represent the public face of hip-hop, especially after they recorded a track for Spike Lee's 1989 movie *Do the Right Thing.*

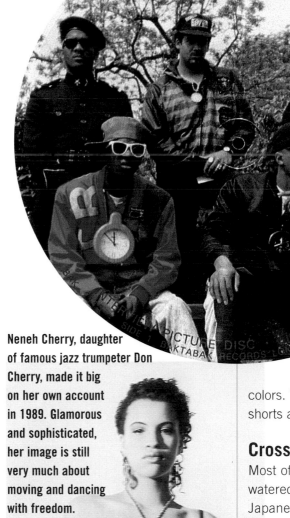

Neneh Cherry, daughter of famous jazz trumpeter Don Cherry, made it big on her own account in 1989. Glamorous and sophisticated, her image is still very much about moving and dancing with freedom.

Adidas, Nike, Reebok sneakers—and knowing which were the labels to be seen in meant being part of the scene yourself. Anything that made it into the magazines was already out of date.

House and After

The edgy sound and jerky dancing of the hip-hop movement had a streetwise, aggressive feel. It reflected the pressures of inner-city life. By the mid-eighties, a new black sound had emerged from Chicago—the House movement. House music drew its inspiration from seventies disco, jazz, or Latin music. Artists and fans preferred to dress up smart, which meant big jackets, *Miami Vice*-style suits. By 1988, House had diversified and was no longer just an American movement. The stylized "vogue-ing" became popular, a dance that resembled a freeze-frame movie. Italy was fast becoming an important center of record production, while in Britain, media attention focused on the Acid House craze, famed as much for the packed, semi-legal warehouse parties and eye-catching fashions as for the music itself.

Acid House looked back to the sixties for many of its ideas—brightly colored or fluorescent tops worn outside loose jeans, pedalpushers, or harem pants in bright "acid" colors. Tie-dye and batik or African-inspired prints mixed in with Lycra cycling shorts and other familiar items from the sportswear shops.

Crossover

Most of these fashions only reached the suburbs and the chain stores in a watered-down form. But like the new shapes of Kawakubo and the other Japanese designers, they made their presence felt in unexpected ways. The eighties obsession with dance and exercise ensured there was always a big following for the latest dance sounds, even those of the less safe and familiar variety.

African American designers were gaining attention for their clothes through the popularity of the music that went with them. By the end of the decade, House and hip-hop had become the single biggest influence on youthful street fashion, while a new generation of recording stars— Adeva, Neneh Cherry, Soul II Soul—looked set to carry their influence into the nineties.

Second Skin: Design in New Fabrics

Workout!

In the 1980s, you had to be fit. Not just thin but fit. Whether you were Madonna or the president, some form of exercise was obligatory—and exercise that hurt and worked those muscles. Aerobic and dance studios, gyms and weight machines sprang up like mushrooms. Exercise books, cassettes, and videotapes sold by the thousands for those too shy to work out in public. Muscles had to be toned, fat burned off, and the body firmed up like an Olympic athlete's. And if you dropped out of your class, at least you could live your fantasies at the movies, with films like *Dirty Dancing* becoming big box office hits.

In Love with Lycra

Once you had the shape, you needed the right clothes to show it off. Suddenly, even brief running shorts looked old hat and baggy. Figure-hugging Lycra looked good and was also better aerodynamically. Florence Griffith-Joyner, better known as Flo-Jo, stunned the world not just with her record-breaking running but with her skintight, brightly colored, one-legged outfits. Lycra shorts became high fashion. So did bicycling, as long as you were a city messenger weaving your way in and out of heavy traffic on an unwieldy mountain bike. Lycra leotards in neon colors were worn not only in the exercise studio but to parties too, with a figure-hugging skirt as cover-up. With Lycra tights coming

onto the market, you could be encased in this wonder fabric from top to toe—very decently covered, but with every curve and ripple of well-worked muscle outlined.

After Lycra, it was a simple step to move on to rubber. Latex, a form of rubber that lets air through, was used first for water sports and swimwear and then for clinging tops, skirts, and shorts. You had to be brave to wear it and to have worked hard at all those classes.

▲Rubber Soul. These Neils Jorgensen designs make use of the cutting and draping possibilities of rubber, as well as its more obvious stretching and clinging qualities.

▶A new shape for the late-eighties mini—wool jersey combined with latex for the Aquagirl look. Argentinian-Australian designer Willy de la Vega also produced a popular range of latex swimwear.

◀ Work that body! When Lycra exercise wear moved out onto the street, the bicycle became the most important exercise accessory.

▲These influential designs by Azzedine Alaïa, king of the "body beautiful," were first seen in 1987.

◄ Olympic gold medal sprinter Florence Griffith-Joyner—popularly known as Flo-Jo—became as famous for her stunning fashion sense on the track as for her record-breaking running at the 1988 Seoul Olympics.

Design-a-Body

For those who wanted the shape but didn't want to look as if they had come straight from the sports field or out of the pool, there was only one top designer. Azzedine Alaïa became a fad in the eighties, although he had been dressing famous women from his studio in Paris for the last thirty years. His artfully constructed dresses of leather and clinging fabrics showed women off to their best advantage, concealing flaws as often as they revealed alluring curves. He combined the flair of street style with the assurance of high fashion to create a powerful look that was very much of the decade. In other hands, the same materials looked tacky, an exercise for the catwalk rather than to be worn in real life.

▲▶Ultra-fashionable couples exercised together in his-and-hers high-fashion Lycra bicyclewear.

Underpinnings

Taut and toned, this ideal body did not need any serious support from wired bras or girdles. It became rather difficult to figure out what was underwear and what should go on top, since sporty-looking shapes were sold as bras and tight leggings worn as pants. It was the shape underneath that counted, and if you didn't have it, you were better off leaving Lycra and latex alone.

Retro Fever

Retreat to the Past

If keeping up with the fast-moving eighties became too hard, the safest thing to do was to sink into an older and better world. The only problem was that the past was moving fast too. If you hadn't changed your wardrobe for ten years, it was more than likely that you would become highly fashionable again.

Fashion nostalgia was certainly nothing new, but in the eighties, it was taken to extremes, with the very recent past being plundered for ideas. The fifties, the swinging sixties, even punk were all revived, with a little something of the present added as well. It might be just in slight touches, like a pair of sixties-style ski pants, or a bizarre total imitation of punk style only a few years after the whole thing had died.

By the end of the decade, even the most forward-looking designers were looking to the past. Yohji Yamamoto's 1989 autumn menswear collection paid homage to the America of the 1950s, with sweaters and zipper jackets inspired by the baseball field, while Yves Saint Laurent was reviving flower power, with loose floral shirts for evening wear. Odd reminders of the past could turn up when least expected, like Jean Paul Gaultier's use of thick-soled Doc Marten boots. Advertisers quickly jumped on the retro bandwagon, using the music and images of previous decades to sell goods to the fashion-conscious youngsters of the eighties.

Rock 'n' Roll Goes On

The continuing popularity of the sounds of the sixties and seventies kept the fashions of those decades alive too. A hard core of people remained who were attached not only to the music of their youth but also to the natural, informal look they had adopted as rebellious teenagers. But some 1980s youngsters also fell for the long hair and ragged, faded jeans look, as well as the music that went with it.

▼The craze for ripped and slashed jeans resurfaced in 1989, proving yet again that in fashion, there's nothing new under the sun.

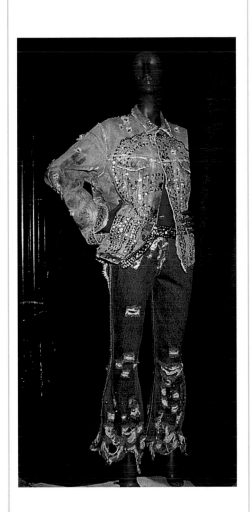

▲ Another retro denim design, this time embellished with fake stones, from British designer Katherine Hamnett in 1989.

▲ By the end of the decade, the rural past was once again providing inspiration to designers like Ralph Lauren and Laura Ashley. City-dwelling customers flocked to dress themselves in clothes that spoke of tradition and old money.

Kid Creole and the Coconuts and the B-52s are just two examples of performers who made use of retro images and fifties typefaces on their album jackets. A whole book could be filled with similar examples.

Throughout the 1980s, the sounds of previous decades kept popping up in the charts. In 1989, Bob Dylan, The Rolling Stones, The Who, The Beach Boys, and Paul McCartney were all touring and releasing new albums. As if in sympathy, fashion saw a brief revival of ethnic-print skirts, deliberately ripped jeans, fringing, and beads, all recalling the era of the Woodstock festival twenty years earlier.

Secondhand Chic

For some people, looking back to the past was a dedicated quest for the quality, style, and cut that they felt contemporary clothes could not provide. Thrift stores, charity stores, and garage sales were all raided for additions to the wardrobe and the home. Anything from horn-rimmed sunglasses to a double-breasted suit of forty years ago could be picked up for considerably less than the latest fashions being sold in the chic department stores. A complete look from a chosen decade could be painstakingly reconstructed in original clothing, but most people looked to the thrift shops to find something cheap and individual that could add just that fashionable touch of the past to their modern wardrobe.

►This Giorgio Armani evening dress looks back to the late sixties for its inspiration. The styling and pose of the model, and the antique jewelry, add to the effect.

▼Yves Saint Laurent launched a range of sixties-style flowery-print shirts for men as well as women.

Towards the Nineties

Prime Time

By the end of the eighties, age was already becoming a dominant factor. In North America and Europe, the demographic was changing, with many more people in the forty-five to sixty-six bracket and fewer sixteen- to twenty-four-year-olds. The traditional youth market was becoming less important. Fashions had to adapt to dressing the "woopie"—the well-off older person who had the money and leisure to spend on expensive clothes and accessories.

President George Bush's wife, Barbara, was already setting the tone. The previous first lady, Nancy Reagan, had always been fashionable, but her wardrobe and pencil-slim figure were modeled on clothes designed for women many years her junior. Barbara Bush's style was elegant but matronly. She proved that you could still look good without pretending to be young. American designers like Donna Karan and Calvin Klein were already providing toned-down grown-up fashions for an older market, both for leisure and for work. European designers, with their greater emphasis on innovation, seemed to be lagging behind.

▲New first lady Barbara Bush brought a new and more relaxed style to the White House in 1989.

►Setting the pace. Informality isn't just for the young—in fact, by the end of the decade fashion had come full circle and the affluent older consumer was as important in the market as the teenager was in the sixties.

▲Rei Kawakubo's 1989 collection abandoned trademark black for a whole new range of floaty garments in pastel colors, all worn with silver wigs.

The last word in formal wear: over the suits go loose-fitting mohair coats with velvet trim, plus, for her, the extra luxury of panne velvet scarf and gloves. Dapper was still the way to be as the eighties gave way to the nineties.

Global Environment

The world was also growing more fragile. The late eighties saw a growing awareness of the damage being done to the environment, and it became more fashionable to be "green" and environmentally aware. This had the greatest impact on beauty products, with the use of ozone-friendly hairsprays, non-animal-tested cosmetics, and fruit- and flower-based oils and scents becoming not just a fashion craze but a social duty.

Shrinking World

Ever-improving communications made the world seem even smaller. With popular American TV series showing in countries all over the world, knowledge of Western fashions spread to the most remote rural areas. But the fashion traffic was by no means one way: shapes, colors, and textile designs were continually imported into the West from other countries as travel became easier and quicker. The traditional fashion centers of Paris, Rome, New York, and London had already had to face up to challenges from Japan and Germany; in the nineties, countries like Spain, Portugal, Australia, and even Turkey would pose a threat.

Good worldwide communications also made the pirating of designs easier. With pictures sent from one country to another at the touch of a button, cheap copies of new ideas could be in clothing stores in a matter of weeks.

In the nineties, fashions would change at a frantic pace.

▲The zipper detail on this sleek hip-length jacket by Donna Karan adds a touch of modernity to a garment designed for the grown-up wardrobe.

▶ Calvin Klein, the essence of cool, wearing clothing from his own collection. His spare, clean shapes and modern lines kept the Calvin Klein brand at the forefront of urban chic well into the next decade.

Chronology

News

1980
Iran–Iraq War breaks out.
New York transit strike.
Moscow stages Olympics.
Ronald Reagan elected US president.

1981
World economic recession.
US hostages released from Iran.
Martial law in Poland.

1982
War in South Atlantic.
Israel invades Lebanon.
Warnings of danger from acid rain.
Time magazine names the computer "Man of the Year".

1983
Margaret Thatcher reelected as British prime minister.

1984
Walter Mondale runs for US president with Geraldine Ferraro but loses to Reagan and Bush.
Ethiopian famine.

1985
Mikhail Gorbachev becomes Soviet premier.
Anglo-Irish agreement on Northern Ireland.

1986
Challenger space shuttle disaster.
Chernobyl nuclear disaster.
UK and France reach agreement to build Channel tunnel.
Irangate scandal in US.

1987
Glasnost (openness) takes off in USSR.
Margaret Thatcher elected for third term as British prime minister.
Stock market crash in October.

1988
End of the Cold War?
Ceasefire in Iran–Iraq War.
George Bush elected US president.
Seoul stages the Olympics.

1989
Massive political change in Eastern Europe.
Berlin Wall breached.
Death of Ayatollah Khomeini.
Tiananmen Square massacre.

Events

The Face begins publication.
Nightclubbing becomes new focus of youth culture.
Dallas reaches 300 million audience worldwide.

Adam Ant *Stand and Deliver* video.
"New Romantic" movement.

Prince has hit with "1999".
Grandmaster Flash popularizes rap with "The Message".

Break-dancing craze.
The term "yuppie" starts to gain wide currency.

Band Aid concert.
Madonna emerges as a megastar.
Boom in dance movies.

Live Aid concert.
AIDS recognized as an epidemic by World Health Organization.

Fashion Aid show.

Hugo Boss suits feature in *LA Law*.
"Yuppie" culture reaches its peak.

Acid House craze widely noted.
Flo-Jo makes big impact at Olympics.

Batman movie.
First lady Barbara Bush promotes a stylish but matronly look for older women.

Fashion

Calvin Klein shirtwaists.
Ralph Lauren "Frontier Fashion" collection.
Vivienne Westwood "Pirate" look.
Karl Lagerfeld revives miniskirts.

Knickers in style.
Rei Kawakubo shows first collection in Paris.
Norma Kamali shows "sweats" collection.

Azzedine Alaïa's first New York show.
Body Map label formed.
Armani shows culottes.

Gaultier's slashed and layered look.
Boom in jogging suits and other exercise wear.
Kawakubo Paris show divides opinion.

Donna Karan founds own label.
Romeo Gigli's "Italian Madonna" look.

Saint Laurent features short skirts, leather garments and cinched-in waists.
Neils Jorgensen, Daniel James, and others show radical garments using rubber and latex in original ways.

Christian Lacroix shows first couture collection.

Lycra, no longer confined to exercise studios, gains wide popularity for leisure and party wear.

Aquagirl produces sporty look in latex and other fabrics.
Retro looks for evening wear from Armani and others.

Ripped jeans fad.
Yamamoto shows fifties Americana collection.
Fabrics come to the fore: paisley, lamé, African prints, lace batiks.

Glossary

Alaïa, Azzedine (dates unknown) French designer, born in Tunisia. Worked for Dior, Mugler, and others before forming his own label in 1982. Famed for his figure-hugging dresses in leather, cashmere, and stretch fabrics.

Aquagirl Swiss-based label formed by Argentinian-Australian designer Willy de la Vega in 1986, originally specializing in Lycra and Latex designs for sports- and beach-wear.

Armani, Giorgio (b. 1935) Italian designer. Formed his own label in 1975. Famous for his suits and jackets, especially the wide-shouldered look for executive women.

Benetton North Italian family firm established in the early sixties by Lucian Benetton. Benetton remained popular throughout the eighties for their colorful casual wear and knitwear separates.

Body Map British design partnership formed in 1982 by David Holal and Stevie Stewart.

Burberry Company founded by Thomas Burberry (1835-1926) in Dorking, England, manufacturing gabardine rain- and sportswear. Company continues to flourish and set standards in this field.

Boss, Hugo (d.1948) German menswear designer. Achieved prominence when his suits were worn by characters in Dallas and *LA Law*.

Comme des Garçons Label formed in 1969 by Rei Kawakubo (b. 1942). Kawakubo's designs attract attention by their muted colors and radical approach to cutting and shaping.

Couture Abbreviation of the French phrase haute couture. Haute couture has in the past meant individually created garments but in recent years, the expression has also been used to refer to limited editions of designer garments.

Coveri, Enrico (1952-1990) Italian designer. Established his own label in 1979. Coveri is famous for his youthful, fun-loving designs.

Doc[tor] Martens Hard-wearing British workingmen's footwear, fashionable with young people in Britain during the eighties.

Emanuel, David and Elizabeth (both b. 1953) British designers, born in Glamorgan, Wales. They shot to prominence as designers of Lady Diana Spencer's dress for the 1981 royal wedding.

Galliano, John (b. 1960) British designer. Broke through to instant fame with his "Les Incroyables" collection of 1984. Innovative and even quirky, Galliano is very popular with the younger buyer.

Gaultier, Jean Paul (b. 1952) French designer. Started his own company in 1977. Now one of the most influential of the French ready-to-wear designers, his work continued to surprise and provoke throughout the eighties.

Gigli, Romeo (dates unknown) Italian designer. Worked for the Callaghan label before forming his own company in 1983. His "Italian Madonna" look of 1984 brought him widespread acclaim.

Hamnett, Katherine (b. 1948) British designer. Established her own business in 1979 becoming particularly successful in the Italian and British markets. Her large-slogan T-shirts created considerable impact in 1984.

Hennes Inexpensive Swedish fashion chain, very active in the younger market in Europe in the late eighties.

Kamali, Norma (b. 1945) American designer, based in New York. Formed her own label in 1978 and received widespread acclaim throughout the eighties for her fashionable sportswear and office wear for the executive woman. Has also been innovative in her approach to fabrics.

Karan, Donna (b. 1948) American designer. Worked for Anne Klein until forming her own label in 1984. Renowned for wearable sportswear and stylish clothes for the mature woman.

Kenzo (b. 1940) Japanese designer. Worked under his own Jap label in Paris from 1970. A successful blender of Eastern and Western styles, Kenzo paved the way for the wider popularity of Japanese designers in the seventies and eighties.

Klein, Calvin (b. 1942) American designer. Started his own business in 1968, initially specializing in suits and coats. His smooth, understated look was a key influence in the eighties, especially in the USA.

Lagerfeld, Karl (b. 1938) German designer, based in Paris. Worked for Chloe, Krizia, and Chanel before launching his own collection in 1984. His imaginative and witty designs remained a major fashion force throughout the 1980s.

Lauren, Ralph (b. 1939) American designer. Worked for several menswear clients before launching his own women's label in 1972. Launched his influential "Prairie" look in 1978, featuring denim skirts worn over layered white petticoats. In the eighties, upheld the tradition of quality fabrics for menswear and womenswear and became a cult designer for the yuppie buyer.

Miyake, Issey (b. 1935) Japanese designer, born in Hiroshima. Worked in Paris from 1965 and with Geoffrey Beene in New York from 1969 before forming his own label in 1971. Extremely influential in the 1980s with his bold cutting and draping, and innovative use of textures and sculptural shapes.

Montana, Claude (b. 1949) French designer. Worked in jewelry and leather before launching a collection of clothing under his own name in 1977. Showed great flair with sportswear as well as leather and remained a consistently influential designer in the eighties.

Mugler, Thierry (b. 1948) French designer. Designing under his own name from 1973, has been a leading exponent of the "hourglass" and figure-hugging fashions of the 1980s, although his clothes are often influenced by fashions of the forties and fifties.

Westwood, Vivienne (b. 1941) British designer. Closely associated with the rise of the punk movement in the 1970s. In 1980 launched her "Pirate" look, which became linked with the contemporary "New Romantic" movement in pop. Continued to produce original and even anarchic collections throughout the eighties, including the "Witches" of 1983 and the "Mini-Crinolines" of 1985.

Yamamoto, Yohji (b. 1943) Japanese designer. Formed his own company in 1972, showing his first collection in Japan in 1976. Uncompromising and anti-traditional, Yamamoto achieved considerable attention with his loose, unstructured, but cleverly cut and swathed black-and-white garments. In the late eighties, began to allow more color in his collections.

Further Reading

Fewer books have so far been published on 1980s fashion than on previous decades, but this is changing. Magazines and films are still excellent sources for further investigation.

Adult General Reference Sources

Calasibetta, Charlotte. *Essential Terms of Fashion: A Collection of Definitions* (Fairchild, 1985)

Calasibetta, Charlotte. *Fairchild's Dictionary of Fashion*, (Fairchild, 2nd ed,1988)

Cumming, Valerie. *Understanding Fashion History* (Chrysalis, 2004)

Ewing, Elizabeth. *History of Twentieth Century Fashion*, revised by Alice Mackrell (Batsford, 4th ed, 2001)

Gold, Annalee. *90 Years of Fashion* (Fairchild, 1990)

Laver, James. *Costume and Fashion* (Thames & Hudson, 1995)

O'Hara, Georgina. *The Encyclopedia of Fashion* (Harry N. Abrams, 1986)

Peacock, John. *Men's Fashion: The Complete Sourcebook* (Emerald, 1997)

Peacock, John. *Fashion Accessories: The Complete 20th Century Sourcebook* (Thames & Hudson, 2000)

Skinner, Tina. *Fashionable Clothing from the Sears Catalogs* (Schiffer, 2004)

Steele, Valerie. *Fifty Years of Fashion: New Look to Now* (Yale, 2000)

Stegemeyer, Anne. *Who's Who in Fashion*, (Fairchild, 4th ed, 2003)

Trahey, Jane (ed.) Harper's Bazaar: *100 Years of the American Female* (Random House, 1967)

Watson, Linda. *Twentieth-century Fashion* (Firefly, 2004)

Young Adult Sources

Lomas, Clare. *Twentieth Century Fashion: the 80s and 90s* (Heinemann Library, 1999)

Wilcox, R. Turner. *Five Centuries of American Costume* (Scribner's, 1963).

Acknowledgments

The Publishers would like to thank the following for permission to reproduce illustrations: Advertising Archive 15; Allsport 13b, 17l, 50l; Bath Museum of Costume 32l, 39r; B.T. Batsford 8l, 9, 17r, 19t, 20t, 22, 25, 26l, 29t, 31l, 32r, 33tl, 34l, 34br, 37r, 42, 43l, 44, 45, 46tl, 46r, 47, 48, 49r, 52, 53r, 54, 55r, 56b, 58; Camera Press 8tr, 8br; Corbis 35, 55l, 59r; Museum at FIT 18, 38, 57; Retro Library 59l; Rex Features 7t, 10t, 11t, 12, 13t, 16l, 20b, 21, 26r, 27, 28, 30, 31r, 33bl, 34tr, 36, 37l, 40, 41, 46bl, 49l, 50r, 51, 53l, 56t; Topfoto 6, 7b, 10b, 11bl, 11br, 14, 16r, 19b, 23, 24, 29b, 33r, 39l

Key: b=bottom, t=top, l=left, r=right

Index

Figures in italics refer to
illustrations.